GOD IS ENOUGH

Shedding whatever it takes to experience a deeper
relationship with self, others and God.

By Kathy B. Dempsey, Founder, The Shedding Revolution™
www.SheddingRevolution.com

GOD IS ENOUGH

By Kathy B. Dempsey

Copyright ©2016

Published by: Trey Press

Photography by: Kathy B. Dempsey, Sunrise Easter Morning in the Sky Above Rome

Printed in the United States of America
ISBN: 978-0-9742926-1-8

Dedication

This journal is dedicated to the memory of my mother, Katie Bleuer, one of the most deeply spiritual women I have ever met.

Growing up, I remember passing by my mother's bedroom every morning and she always was in one spot — on her knees praying to God.

Being spiritual was not what she did; it was who she was!

Bless you Naomi Rhode, my heart mom.

And a special thanks to Jamie Rasmussen who was the catalyst that God used allowing me to heal and spiritually SHED.

Your Shedding Journey

You are invited you to join me in a shedding journey. A time of exploration, daily reflection, and insights that will deepen your relationship with self, others, and God.

My prayer is that this endeavor will be an incredible spiritual awakening for you.

Let me introduce you to what has become my personal philosophy of life by sharing my journal entry dated July 29, 1998:

It was 7 a.m. Time for our quarterly Ethics meeting at the hospital. As I rushed into the room at the last minute, I ran into a guy, David Mann, I hadn't seen in a while. "Good morning, David, and how are you?"

"I am fine, Kathy, … but my lizard is dead."

Startled yet intrigued, I asked, "Your lizard is dead! What happened?"

"He didn't shed his skin…and if lizards don't shed their skin, they die."

"Why?" I asked.

He explained. "Lizards grow by shedding their skin. If they don't shed their skin, they aren't growing. Lizards die if they don't grow."

After I thought for a moment, I said, "David, what can we learn from the lizard?"

With a perplexed look on his face, he replied, "We all need to grow, we need to grow physically, mentally, spiritually … and how we grow is to shed our old skin. If we don't grow as humans, we'll die."

"And, David, what does our old skin represent? Maybe old habits? Negative thoughts? Unhealthy relationships?"

Simultaneously, we looked at each other…the light bulb had gone on. "Shed or you're dead!"

Two things happened that day. First, it gave me a benchmark for my personal growth. Second, because God had put David in my path that day, I had a metaphor — "Shed or You're Dead®," with Lenny the Lizard, who soon would become my life's companion and my personal vehicle for helping others grow physically, mentally and spiritually.

Lenny has observed humans and has noticed that sometimes they get stuck and are unable to let go of things that are holding them back in life. Often times people refuse to detach themselves from relationships or situations even if they are causing them great harm.

The concept of shedding is not new. The Apostle Paul says, "This one thing I do, forgetting those things which are behind, and reaching forth unto those things which are before. I press toward the mark for the prize of the high calling of God in Christ Jesus." (Philippians 3:13-14)

As Apostle Paul said this ONE thing I do — SHED®!

Shedding is about letting go of the old and embracing the new.

Lenny's Challenge: Are you willing to do whatever it takes to SHED and experience a deeper relationship with God? Yes, I am. I take the Pledge to SHED. _____.

SIGNATURE

Congratulations! You are ready to begin the journey! Take 60 seconds and ask yourself:

What is your old skin?

_____

_____

What has been holding you back in life?

_____

_____

What might you become if you SHED the old skin?

_____

_____

My Shedding Journey

In the mid-80s, I experienced a life-changing event in which I was the first healthcare worker in the United States to be diagnosed HIV positive. I would invite you to read, *Shed or You're Dead®: 31 Unconventional Strategies for Change and Growth* to read about how this traumatic event turned out and how it changed my life.

Because of my AIDS incident, I felt called in August 2005 to go to Africa and volunteered for a month in Zambia with orphans who had all lost their parents to AIDS. Little did I realize I would experience a journey that would forever transform and deepen my relationship with God. My traumatic experiences prior to arriving in Africa were God's way of preparing me for learning my greatest life lesson:

GOD IS ENOUGH

Throughout the journal you will find the spiritual lessons I internalized during my journey to Africa. While volunteering in Zambia, I witnessed the unimaginable - how the devasting conditions of poverty, malnutrition and lack of education were affecting thousands of children. I saw kids who had lost both parents to AIDS and now were the heads of households, children dying in the middle of the streets, 14-year olds who had never attended a day of school. This humbling experience was a wake-up call for me to SHED. The stark reality is we will lose everything and everyone that we love in life. The only thing we have 100% assurance of is that God will be there for us and He will never leave us. After you read the lessons throughout the journal, I encourage you to take some time to reflect and respond to Lenny's challenge.

Suggestions for Journaling

• Pick a quiet place to be alone. Consider creating a small area in your home that is your sacred space.

• Pick a time of day that works best for you. Early morning or before bed are good times. I do both.

• The focus of your shedding journey is to focus on ONE passage of scripture that has ONE message: SHED! (Philippians 3:13-14) Go at your own pace. What feels right for you, whether it be 10 days or 10 weeks.

• As you continue to journal, read each spiritual lesson. Take 60 seconds to reflect on Lenny's challenge, then record your thoughts, feelings and insights for the day.

• End your journal entry with four things:

　1. **What are my affirmations?** *We become what we think about. We become what we visualize. Our brains believe what we tell it. Examples: I am loved by God. God is enough. His grace is sufficient. I am a gift of God. I am healthy and whole. I SHED whatever it is that is holding me back.*

　2. **What is the lesson learned?** *What did you learn today? Every experience, every relationship is an opportunity to learn and grow. If we don't stop to reflect, sometimes we miss the lesson and have to learn it again the hard way.*

　3. **What am I grateful for?** *So often we get stuck in negative thinking about how difficult and stressed our life has become. Identifying what you are grateful for will help remind you how blessed you are.*

　4. **What is my prayer list?** *For who? About what?*

About my Personal Shedding

When you hear the words spiritually shedding, you think …

_____

_____

_____

The most significant thing that has helped you to grow spiritually has been …

_____

_____

_____

When you think about someone close to God, you think about (who)… because (why) …

_____

_____

_____

If you were closer to God, you would …

_____

_____

_____

You feel closest to God when you are …

_____

_____

_____

The one thing that you could do to draw closer to God is to ...

_____

_____

_____

The biggest barrier to drawing closer to God is ...

_____

_____

_____

The one question you would like to ask God is ...

_____

_____

_____

GOD IS ENOUGH means ...

_____

_____

_____

On a scale of 1-10. (1 being low and 10 being high) how unconditionally do you love yourself? What would make it a 10?

_____

_____

On a scale of 1-10. (1 being low and 10 being high) how unconditionally do you love others? What would make it a 10?

_____

_____

Drawing Challenge (Part I): Draw a picture of your vision of what you would like your relationship with God to be like. Resist the urge to use any words.

Drawing Challenge (Part II): On this page, draw a picture of your current relationship with God. Resist the urge to use any words.

Draw a spiritual graph of your life. Starting with birth at the bottom left corner and move horizontally across the page until you get to your current age. The vertical axis goes from 1 to 10. (1 being no relationship with God. 10 being in blissful communion.) Without any judgment, plot out the significant life events throughout your life and the correlation to your relationship to God.

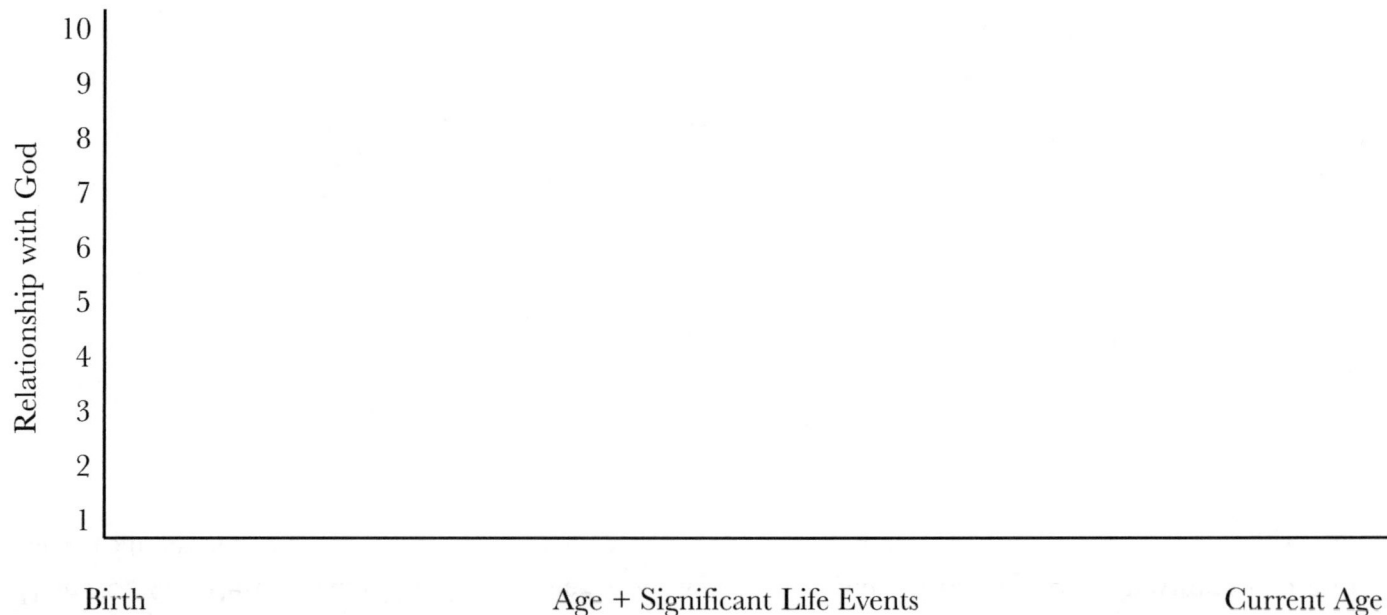

Relationship with God

10
9
8
7
6
5
4
3
2
1

Birth   Age + Significant Life Events   Current Age

Letter to God

Now that you have done the drawing challenge and your spiritual graph,
take 10 minutes and write a letter to God.

_____

_____

_____

_____

_____

_____

_____

_____

Lesson 1

Realizing your true valuables lie inside of you.

Amsterdam — the perfect place to rest and break up the long 10,000 mile trip to Africa. Or so I thought! After visiting the famous Anne Frank house, I roamed down streets, canal after canal. Thinking this may be the last time I'd be able to check email, I darted into an Internet cafe, unsnapped my backpack belt from around my waist, carefully placed my bag under my chair and sat down to work. Suddenly, I looked around and my backpack was gone!

My heart sank into the pit of my stomach as my psyche began to catalog what had vanished — my passport, all my money, my credit cards, my bank cards, my travelers' checks, my camera, my video camera, my medications, my jewelry, my itinerary, my plane tickets, my lizard key chain complete with keys and my precious 2005 journal.

With horror, I admitted to myself the unthinkable — a thief had snatched my bag from between my legs. The culprit had even stolen my map of Amsterdam along with the name of the hotel in which I was staying and my hotel room key. I pleaded with the cafe clerk to call the police. He grunted and refused, touting, "They won't come! There are too many pickpockets around here. You will have to go to find the police yourself." Stunned with his response, I wandered outside into the cool, breezy night. Feeling unhinged from everything and everybody on Earth, I stood in the middle of the dark street and struggled to stop the tears from flowing. What was I going to do? I didn't even have any money to make a phone call.

In just more than 24 hours, my flight was leaving for Africa. I was alone, LOST in Amsterdam, with NOTHING but the clothes on my back!

Lenny has observed humans and has realized that humans too often depend on their "stuff" to anchor them. People tend to define their self-sufficiency by how much money they have or the possessions they own. In reality, our possessions are all an illusion. At any moment we can be stripped of everything. Real self-sufficiency comes from realizing that our true valuables lie inside ourselves. Remember that whatever happens to us externally, no one can take away our Divine spirit within.

Lenny's Challenge: You are created in the image of God and no one can take away the divine in you. Realizing your true valuables lie inside of you is 100 percent your choice! Shed or You're Dead®! Take 60 seconds and ask yourself:

How do you define your self-sufficiency?

_____

_____

More externally or internally based?

_____

_____

What would you do if all your external valuables were taken away?

_____

_____

How would you react?

_____

_____

What feelings would you have?

_____

_____

What is something you can do this week to remind yourself that true valuables are not what you have but who you are inside.

_____

_____

As a reminder, take a few minutes to answer the four critical questions that follow each lesson.

What are my affirmations?

_____

_____

_____

_____

_____

What is the lesson learned?

_____

_____

_____

_____

_____

What am I grateful for?

_____

_____

_____

_____

_____

What is my prayer list?

_____

_____

_____

_____

_____

Lesson 2

Trusting God to open the right doors.

As I stood all alone with nothing but the clothes on my back in the middle of a dark Amsterdam street, questions flooded my mind. "What do I do? Where do I go? How do I find the police?" I didn't have a penny to my name. I faintly remembered the cafe clerk rambling something about the police station being three blocks down, then make a left ... about 15 minutes down the road. Confused about what to do, I just started walking. Trying to protect myself from the cutting wind, I pulled up the hood to my jacket. If only I had my gloves, I thought, but they were in the backpack, too!

I knew I had made a wrong turn when I found myself smack in the middle of Amsterdam's famous "Red Light" district. I had never witnessed such sights — women hanging out of windows. I knew they had money but I was not about to stop and ask them for help.

Once again, I found myself seeking direction. I walked into a small corner store, but no one seemed to pay me much attention so I walked back out. Then I looked back to the sign. It was an exotic mushroom store, better known in Amsterdam as a marijuana house!

Things seemed to be getting worse as the night went on. I had to find the police. I had to keep walking.

Fortunately, from a distance, I saw a large sign — POLICE STATION — at the end of the block. I was ecstatic! Finally, after two hours of searching, I MADE IT!! With a renewed spark, I picked up the pace and ran to the door. I grabbed the handle and pulled. But the door wouldn't open. I jerked the handle back and forth, thinking it was stuck, but it wouldn't budge. I pounded on the door. Finally I let go, stepped back and allowed my eyes to read the sign on the door. POLICE STATION CLOSED!

Police Station Closed?!? How could a police station close? (Well, think about it. Just about everything in Amsterdam is legal, so why do they need the police?)

Lenny has witnessed humans and has noticed that throughout life, people are often confronted with closed doors. Sometimes it's a job, a relationship, a deal which falls through - something doesn't work out as planned. In desperation, we often keep beating the closed door, hoping it will open. As difficult as closed doors are to accept, we must ultimately keep our eyes wide open and move towards the next open door. Some of life's best lessons are found when a door closes and we are forced to seek out new open doors.

Lenny's Challenge: When God closes a door, he often opens a window! Trusting God to open the right doors is 100 percent your choice! Shed or You're Dead®! Take 60 seconds and ask yourself:

What closed doors are you running into in your life right now?

_____

_____

Where do you keep beating on doors, expecting them to open?

_____

_____

Where do you feel stuck trying to make something happen that just won't budge?

_____

_____

What can you do today to let go, trust God, and look for a new open door?

_____

_____

What are my affirmations?

_____

_____

_____

_____

_____

What is the lesson learned?

_____

_____

_____

_____

_____

What am I grateful for?

_____

_____

_____

_____

_____

What is my prayer list?

_____

_____

_____

_____

_____

3
Lesson

Realizing we are all beggars before God.

The Amsterdam Police Station closed?!? In disbelief I wondered, "How can a police station close?" What should I do now? It was 10 p.m., dark and no one was around. I was exhausted, thirsty and had not a penny to my name. I convinced myself to keep moving, keep walking and keep looking for help. As I headed back down the street, a beggar approached me. Feeling bombarded after being approached by beggars several times that day, I quickly snapped back. "I have NO money. Leave me alone!" I looked disgustingly at him and walked away.

My parched tongue craved water. The more I watched people at the sidewalk cafes drinking, the more consumed I became with quenching my thirst. If only I had some change to buy a drink. Finally, I walked into a restaurant. The waitress greeted me, "Table for one?"

"No, I have no money. But please, I need your help. I'm so thirsty and tired. Can I just sit down for a few minutes and rest? Can I please have a glass of water?" I pleaded.

As the words blurted out from my cotton-tongued mouth, I realized the unthinkable. I was now the beggar!

Desperately, I wanted to deny it. I wanted to rationalize and explain to myself how I was different from the beggars on the street. I didn't want to be identified with them. I wanted to judge and say they were panhandlers and I was a victimized American. With tears rolling down my face, I knew in my heart that there was no difference. In reality, aren't we all beggars? Aren't we all trying to get our needs met?

Lenny's Challenge: Realizing we're all beggars before God is 100 percent your choice! Shed or You're Dead®! Take 60 seconds and ask yourself:

"What am I begging for right now?"

_____

_____

In the quiet still moments of your life, what unmet needs do you have?

_____

_____

How are you getting your needs met?

_____

_____

Where do you have a tendency to stand in judgment of others?

_____

_____

Where do you see yourself in the unacceptable actions of others?

_____

_____

Where do you truly hunger and thirst for God? If so, in what way?

_____

_____

What does hungering and thirsting for God mean to you?

_____

_____

What are my affirmations?

_____

_____

_____

_____

_____

What is the lesson learned?

_____

_____

_____

_____

_____

What am I grateful for?

_____

_____

_____

_____

_____

What is my prayer list?

_____

_____

_____

_____

_____

Lesson 4

Asking God for guidance and direction.

The waitress smiled and responded kindly, "Sit here and rest for a few minutes. I will get you a glass of water." I explained my plight — how my bag was stolen with all my valuables inside and that I had no money, no identification and no idea what hotel I was staying in. Despite the restaurant being packed like a can of sardines, she listened intently and suggested, "The chef is from Amsterdam and knows this city inside and out. Let me see if he can come out and help."

In less than two minutes, a guy in white chef hat and apron magically appeared before me. We began to talk. I remembered I was staying at a Best Western hotel. He pulled out the phone book and found that there were six different ones. Based on my description, he immediately pinpointed mine. On a napkin, he drew a map of how to get to my hotel. I pulled my coat hood up and waded back out into the cool night breeze. Finally, I had some clear direction to guide me.

Lenny has observed humans and has noticed that quite often they wander around in life not knowing where they are going. Many times people can't even identify where they are ultimately heading, let along have clear directions and a path to get there. They often are stubborn and think they can do it on their own. They don't need God. Discovering your life's path comes from stopping and taking the time to ask God for guidance.

Lenny's Challenge: Asking God for guidance and direction is 100 percent your choice! Shed or You're Dead®! Take 60 seconds and ask yourself:

Where are you heading in your life right now?

_____

_____

Where do you feel like you keep wandering around trying to figure it out on your own?

_____

_____

What can you do this week to stop, reflect and ask God for guidance and direction in your life?

_____

_____

What are my affirmations?

_____

_____

_____

_____

_____

What is the lesson learned?

_____

_____

_____

_____

_____

What am I grateful for?

_____

_____

_____

_____

_____

_____

What is my prayer list?

_____

_____

_____

_____

_____

_____

5
Lesson

Waiting upon God for renewed strength.

In less than 15 minutes, the chef's primitive napkin directions led me right back to my hotel. As my eyes finally landed on the familiar sign that I'd left 15 hours earlier, I charged through the front door, ran up to the front desk and declared, "I need help!" The front desk clerk stood patiently and listened to my tragic story of all my valuables being stolen at the Internet cafe and how I searched for more than two hours for the police. He responded, "The closest police station that's open is about 15 minutes away. You need to take a taxi." Close to hyperventilating and with tears rolling down my face, I blurted out, "A taxi? I don't have a penny to my name!"

Distracted by someone calling him from the back office, the clerk turned around and said, "Please wait, I'll be right back."

Wait? I'll be right back?

Lenny has observed humans and has noticed that sometimes it is hard for people to wait. In our instant gratification society, we've grow accustomed to demanding things — now! Most of us become impatient if we don't have high-speed Internet access or if we have to wait two minutes at the fast food drive-through line. Whether it's waiting for a phone call, test results, job offer or a relationship response, we tend to spend countless amounts of energy reacting. Waiting can be a renewal gift if we allow ourselves to accept the wait, resist reacting to it and take a much needed breath. God says those who wait upon Him will find renewed strength. (Isaiah 40:31)

Lenny's Challenge: Waiting upon God for renewed strength is 100 percent your choice! Shed or You're Dead®! Take 60 seconds and ask yourself:

How do you respond when you have to wait? Angry? Upset? Worried?

_____

_____

What happens when things don't happen as quickly as you would like? On a scale of 1-10 (1-low, 10-high) how impatient would you rate yourself ?

_____

_____

Do you wait upon God? What does it mean to wait?

_____

_____

Have you ever thought about seeing waiting as a gift from God?

_____

_____

What is one thing you can do to resist the urge to react and wait upon God more in your life?

_____

_____

What are my affirmations?

_____

_____

_____

_____

_____

What is the lesson learned?

_____

_____

_____

_____

_____

What am I grateful for?

_____

_____

_____

_____

_____

What is my prayer list?

_____

_____

_____

_____

_____

6

Lesson

Truly knowing God is Enough!

While I was waiting for the front desk clerk to return, another gentleman stepped up to the counter and said, "I have a message for you, Ms. Dempsey." He handed me an 8x11 sheet of white paper. I unfolded the sheet of paper. It was a faxed message from one of my dear friends, Grace Brame. Noticeably, the sparse message had only three words to it.

GOD IS ENOUGH!

Those three words pierced my soul. I stood at the front desk with tears continuing to run down my face. I had lost everything. I had no money, no identification and no valuables. At the core of my being, I knew God was sending me my biggest life lesson to learn — Despite whatever happens in life, He is enough! I finally got it!

Lenny has observed humans and has noticed that they don't really understand the magnitude of these three simple words. GOD IS ENOUGH. Most of us want to believe GOD IS ENOUGH but we continue to struggle with all of our life attachments.

Lenny's Challenge: Truly believing GOD IS ENOUGH is 100 percent your choice! Shed or You're Dead®! Take 60 seconds and ask yourself:

What does the phrase GOD IS ENOUGH mean to you?

_____

_____

On a scale of 1-10 (1 being low and 10 being high) do you really believe GOD IS ENOUGH? What would make it a 10?

_____

_____

How does your life demonstrate this belief?

_____

_____

In what ways does your life not demonstrate this belief?

_____

_____

What can you do different to more fully live out GOD IS ENOUGH in your daily life?

_____

_____

What are my affirmations?

_____

_____

_____

_____

_____

What is the lesson learned?

_____

_____

_____

_____

_____

_____

What am I grateful for?

_____

_____

_____

_____

_____

What is my prayer list?

_____

_____

_____

_____

_____

_____

7
Lesson

Planning for life's "what ifs."

The five-minute wait allowed me to stop crying and to slow down my breathing. The front desk clerk returned, placed 100 Euros ($120 U.S. dollars) in my hand and said, "I hope this helps." Overwhelmed by his generosity, I thanked him.

He went on, "I have some good news. Your checked baggage (the one that had never arrived from the flight from Philadelphia with my clothes) has been found."

As he pulled out my red suitcase, I remembered that my travel savvy neighbor, Sue Wilson, had insisted I make copies of my passport, credit cards, travelers' checks, itinerary, plane tickets, medication and emergency contacts and put them in my checked baggage. At the time, I was irritated with her suggestion and thought it was a waste of time. Thank God for Sue's words about preparing for a "what if."

Lenny has observed humans and has noticed that people don't often take the time to plan for life's "what ifs." They often see the extra tasks as useless and a waste of time. Often just taking a few extra minutes to ask yourself, "What if?" can help you recover quicker when faced with a crisis. Some people give excuses not to plan and say, "Oh, I will just trust God. God has given us a sound mind and planning skills so don't forget to use them!"

Lenny's Challenge: Planning for life's "what ifs" is 100 percent your choice! Shed or You're Dead®! Take 60 seconds and ask yourself:

Do you currently take time to plan for an unexpected crisis in your life? If not, why?

_____

_____

When was the last time you stopped and asked, "What if?"

_____

_____

What if you lose your job? What if you get sick? What if your computer crashes?

_____

_____

What can you do today to plan for life's "what ifs?" Build an emergency fund. Buy a disability policy. Back up your computer files.

_____

_____

What are my affirmations?

_____

_____

_____

_____

_____

What is the lesson learned?

_____

_____

_____

_____

_____

_____

What am I grateful for?

_____

_____

_____

_____

_____

What is my prayer list?

_____

_____

_____

_____

_____

Lesson 8

Remembering to connect with God daily.

I grabbed the copies of my credit card info out of my suitcase and quickly called to cancel all my credit cards. Then I hopped in a cab and headed to the police station. I stopped at the only pharmacy that was still open. I was amazed they immediately filled six of my stolen prescriptions without question.

When I arrived at the police station, the officer allowed me two phone calls, one to my sister, Virginia, and one to my pastor, Fred. "It's me; I'm in the Amsterdam police station." (I know what they must have been thinking: "Kathy, everything is legal in Amsterdam, what you could have possibly done to get arrested?!?")

After hours of filling out forms, the police drove me back to the hotel. It was 3 a.m. ... and I collapsed. I semi-slept for four hours then jumped out of bed and used my last Euro to take a bus to the U.S. Embassy. There were a dozen people gathered outside the gigantic 20 foot tall black iron gates.

I pushed the gate call button and waited. Finally a guard in full military dress arrived and asked, "Can I help you?"

I responded thankfully, "Yes, I need help. I'm on my way to Africa and my bags were stolen and I need a passport."

His mechanical voice inquired, "Do you have an appointment?"

In shock, I blurted out, "No, I wasn't planning on needing an emergency passport."

Sternly he responded, "We can't help you if you don't have an appointment."

Stunned by his heartless response, emotionally, I began to spiral from hope to despair. OK, I had a meltdown! Grabbing the cold black iron bars and rattling them for dear life, I began hysterically screaming, "What do you mean you can't help me? I am an American! You are the American Embassy!!! I'm all alone, stranded in a foreign country with NO identification or money! I BEG YOU -- PLEASE HELP ME!!!"

Lenny has observed humans and has noticed that sometimes people allow themselves to be rattled by others. Often, we allow someone else's agenda to "rattle our cage." Maybe they didn't listen. Maybe they have a job to do. Maybe they don't care. It's frustrating to realize that people may not always be there for us. We can rest assure in knowing that whatever happens to us, we can access God at any time. No need for an appointment. He will always be there to help us. Sometime we forget that He desires for us to have a close relationship with him daily, not just in times of crisis.

Lenny's Challenge: Remembering to access God daily is 100 percent your choice! Shed or You're Dead®! Take 60 seconds and ask yourself:

Who do you allow to rattle your cage?

_____

_____

How do you react when someone isn't responding to your needs?

_____

_____

Do you realize that while humans may continue to disappoint us, God is always there?

_____

_____

We need no appointment to get help from God? When do you seem to access God most? Just in crisis? Do you use God as your emergency 911 call?

_____

_____

What can you do today to build a closer ongoing relationship with God?

_____

_____

What are my affirmations?

_____

_____

_____

_____

_____

What is the lesson learned?

_____

_____

_____

_____

_____

What am I grateful for?

_____

_____

_____

_____

_____

What is my prayer list?

_____

_____

_____

_____

_____

Lesson 9

Learning life lessons the first time around.

The American Embassy now had a PR crisis right outside their front gates. An hysterical American woman begging for help! It was amazing how quickly they responded to their dilemma and opened the door. "Come on in, ma'am. Calm down, stop crying, we will help you."

In less than three hours, I was handed an emergency passport and was on my way. American Express (yes, don't leave home without them!) immediately gave me replacement travelers' checks and a credit card.

Then Delta's frequent-flyer system electronically located my ticket and I made my scheduled flight to Africa! I took a deep breath and gave a sigh of relief as the plane took off.

Ten hours later, when the plane touched African ground, I cheered. I made it! I hopped off the plane and immediately proceeded to the immigration line. As I stepped up to the counter and handed the official my emergency passport, he said, "Your visa will be $25." I handed him my credit card. "No good." I handed him a travelers' check. "No good, ma'am." I asked him where I could exchange money. "There isn't anywhere. Step aside," he said as he walked away.

Little did I realize what was going on, but the African immigration officials were making arrangements to send me back on the plane. I could feel it coming on ... Meltdown No. 2! Yes, not 24 hours had passed and again my cage was being rattled!

I pleaded, "No, you can't put me back on the plane. I have come too far. All my valuables have been stolen. I am here to help your people and work with the orphans. A taxi cab driver is supposed to be picking me up here. I beg you; please don't send me back on the plane!"

Nothing I was saying or doing was making any difference. They were not going to let me into Africa.

Lenny has observed humans and has noticed sometimes people fail to learn the lesson the first, second or third time around. In fact, life has a way of continuing to present us with similar "learning opportunities" until we finally open our eyes, respond differently and learn the life lesson.

Lenny's Challenge: Learning life lessons the first time around is 100 percent your choice! Shed or You're Dead®! Take 60 seconds and ask yourself:

What experiences in life do you keep experiencing over and over again?

_____

_____

Looking back, what patterns do you see yourself repeating?

_____

_____

Where do you find yourself frequently being taken advantage of?

_____

_____

Where do the same type of individuals continue to show up in your life and what is the lesson to be learned?

_____

_____

How do people continue to treat you the same way over and over again?

_____

_____

What lesson is still unresolved?

_____

_____

What can you do to learn the lesson put in your path as a learning opportunity to know GOD IS ENOUGH?

_____

_____

Now that you have learned the lesson, how will this change your life?

_____

_____

What are my affirmations?

_____

_____

_____

_____

_____

What is the lesson learned?

_____

_____

_____

_____

_____

What am I grateful for?

_____

_____

_____

_____

_____

What is my prayer list?

_____

_____

_____

_____

_____

Lesson 10

Accepting God's gift of amazing grace.

Despite my begging and pleading, nothing I was saying or doing was making any difference. Because of my inability to pay for the visa, the African immigration officials refused to let me into Africa! They didn't care that all my valuables had been stolen.

After an hour of crying and questioning about how I could have come 10,000 miles only to be sent back home, the unexpected happened. A taxi cab driver paid my way into Africa!!! A complete stranger — someone I had didn't even know. If it wasn't for the generous, unexpected gift of this man, I would have been put back on the plane and never been able to help the African orphans.

Lenny has observed humans and has noticed that sometimes they think life is about doing something to get something. Our society is built on merit. But that is not how God works. Nothing I could do or say would get me into Africa. It was a gift … from a stranger. And nothing you can do or say that can get you into heaven. It is a gift … a precious gift from God. It's truly amazing grace!

"For by grace are ye saved through faith; and that not of yourselves: it is the gift of God: Not of works, lest any man should boast." (Ephesians 2:8-9)

Lenny's Challenge: Accepting God's gift of amazing grace is 100 percent your choice! Shed or You're Dead®! Take 60 seconds and ask yourself:

Do you know that God's grace is unwavering?

_____

_____

What will it take for you to know you are perfect in God's eyes?

_____

_____

You are now the taxi cab driver. What unexpected gift of God's grace will you give someone today?

_____

_____

What are my affirmations?

_____

_____

_____

_____

_____

What is the lesson learned?

_____

_____

_____

_____

_____

What am I grateful for?

_____

_____

_____

_____

_____

_____

What is my prayer list?

_____

_____

_____

_____

_____

_____

God's grace is sufficient for me!

— II Corinthians 12:9

SHED EVALUTION & ACTION PLAN

Now that you have completed these 10 lessons, what are your key learnings:

-

-

-

-

-

What is your RX for your personal Shedding Revolution?

Start:

Stop:

Continue:

Congratulations! Happy Shedding!

About Kathy B. Dempsey

Kathy B. Dempsey, award winning author, keynote speaker, and change expert is President of Keep Shedding! Inc. and Founder of The Shedding Revolution. Kathy and her partner Lenny the Lizard, ignite people and organizations with the skills and motivation to lead and manage change.

Kathy is the author of 6 books. Her most popular book, *Shed or You're Dead®: 31 Unconventional Strategies for Change and Growth,* is the recipient of a Writer's Digest International Book Award. Her newest Survival Guide books: *A Fast Acting Change RX for Every Employee and Manager & Healthcare Professional* are considered the go-to guides for many companies. She is also a contributing author for two of the *New York Times Best-selling Chicken Soup for the Soul Series* including *Chicken Soup for the Christian Soul 2.*

Kathy is the editor of *60 Seconds of Shedding,* a monthly e-newsletter read by over 15,000 people worldwide. She has achieved the highest earned speaker's designation in the world, the Certified Speaking Professional (CSP).

A native of Washington, D.C., Kathy now resides in Scottsdale, AZ.

Partial list of clients:

Corporate:
- American Express
- Delta Air Lines
- Disney
- Honeywell
- Nestle
- IBM
- Procter & Gamble
- Shell Oil
- Verizon Wireless
- Wells Fargo

Healthcare:
- Alive Hospice
- American Cancer Society
- American Red Cross
- Bayer
- Catholic Health Initiatives
- Cedars-Sinai Medical Center
- DaVita
- Florida Hospital System
- Geisinger Health System
- Inova Health System
- Johnson & Johnson
- Loma Linda University Health
- Mayo Clinic
- MEDITECH
- Michigan Hospital Association
- Ministry Health Care
- National Kidney Foundation
- Norton Healthcare System
- Parkland Hospital
- Scottsdale Healthcare
- Virginia Organization of Nurse Executives
- Washington Hospital Center

Pharmaceuticals
- Allergan
- GSK
- Pfizer
- Roche
- Sanofi

Faith Based:
- Concord United Methodist Church
- First Baptist Church
- First and Central Presbyterian Church
- Habitat for Humanity
- Presbyterian Church of the Covenant
- Our Lady of the Lake
- St Paul's Episcopal Church
- St. Mark's Lutheran Church

For more resources or to sign up for The Shedding Revolution please visit:

www.SheddingRevolution.com

Kathy B. Dempsey
Founder, The Shedding Revolution
10080 E. Mountain View Lake Dr, Suite 362
Scottsdale, AZ 85258